www. c vlga.org Browsit

Downloadit

← mobile app

IN COLOR

THE 1980s

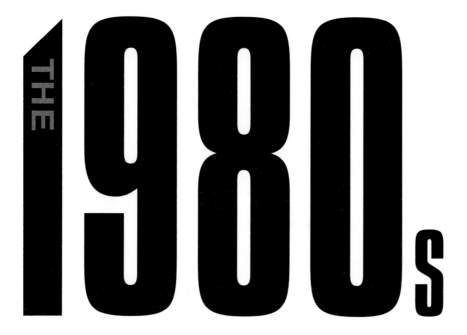

FROM RONALD REAGAN TO MTV **REVISED EDITION**

STEPHEN FEINSTEIN

Library of Congress Cataloging-in-Publication Data

Feinstein, Stephen.
    The 1980s from Ronald Reagan to MTV / Stephen Feinstein.—Rev. ed.
        p. cm. — (Decades of the 20th century in color)
    Includes index.
    ISBN-10: 0-7660-2638-8
    1. Nineteen eighties—Juvenile literature. 2. United States—History—1969– —Juvenile literature. 3. Popular culture—United States—History—20th century—Juvenile literature. 4. United States—Social life and customs—1971– —Juvenile literature. I. Title. II. Series.
    E876.F45 2006
    973.927—dc22
                                                    2005019876
    ISBN-13: 978-0-7660-2638-4

Printed in the United States of America

10 9 8 7 6 5 4 3 2

To Our Readers: We have done our best to make sure all Internet addresses in this book were active and appropriate when we went to press. However, the author and the publisher have no control over and assume no liability for the material available on those Internet sites or on other Web sites they may link to. Any comments or suggestions can be sent by e-mail to comments@enslow.com or to the address on the back cover.

Illustration Credits: AP/Wide World Photos, pp. 4, 9, 20, 21, 23, 24, 25, 32–36, 41–43, 45, 46, 48, 54; Centers for Disease Control, p. 57; Corel Corporation, pp. 22, 30, 39; Enslow Publishers, Inc., pp. 6, 7, 14–17, 31, 58; Everett Collection, Inc., pp. 26–29; JupiterImages Corporation, pp. 10–13, 19, 38; National Aeronautics and Space Administration (NASA), p. 56; USGS/Cascades Volcano Observatory, p. 52.

All interior collages composed by Enslow Publishers, Inc. Images used are courtesy of the previously credited rights holders.

Cover Illustration: AP/Wide World Photos / Corel Corporation / National Aeronautics and Space Administration (NASA).

Contents

The election of Ronald Reagan as U.S. President in 1980 seemed to usher in a newfound sense of optimism for the decade ahead.

Introduction

Compared with the 1960s and 1970s, the decade of the 1980s in the United States was a very different time. During those two earlier decades, many Americans, especially the younger generation, had come to question the values that previous generations had taken for granted. The 1960s had been a time of heroic struggle for civil rights. It had also been a time of urban rioting and the assassinations of President John F. Kennedy, his brother Robert Kennedy, Dr. Martin Luther King, Jr., and Malcolm X. The social upheavals in the 1960s brought about by the Vietnam War and opposition to it continued into the 1970s. Americans in the 1970s also witnessed the sorry spectacle of the Watergate scandal and President Richard Nixon's resignation from office. And the 1970s ended with the humiliating episode of Americans being held hostage in Iran.

By 1980, it was time for a change. Americans were tired of political protests. They were eager to feel good about themselves and their country again. Sensing their mood, Ronald Reagan campaigned for president on the theme of renewing good feelings about America. Thus began the 1980s.

Those who could afford it spent hours in malls (above) or using their credit cards to buy products directly from television via home shopping—a new trend in the 1980s that would become part of the lifestyle of many Americans.

Shop Till You Drop

During the 1980s, shopping malls, which had first become popular in the suburban United States in the 1970s, continued to spread. Americans could now visit shopping malls in cities as well as in small towns. Banks were eager to distribute credit cards to consumers. By the mid-1980s, the average credit-card holder carried seven cards. The easy credit, of course, resulted in an explosion of consumer debt. People flocked to stores and malls. In one six-year period during the mid-1980s, American consumers bought 62 million microwave ovens, 63 million VCRs, 57 million washers and dryers, 105 million color television sets, 31 million cordless phones, and 30 million telephone answering machines. During these same years, Americans also bought 88 million cars and light trucks.

Going to the mall became the favorite leisure-time activity of many Americans. But shopping did not stop at the mall. When they got home, Americans turned on their televisions. Two of the most popular television channels were all about shopping—QVC and the Home Shopping Network. Now, people did not have to leave their homes to buy the products they wanted. They could call in and purchase items they saw on television, using their credit cards.

The Year of the Yuppie

In order to keep on buying, Americans of the 1980s became more focused than ever on how to make money. Many of those who were in college, or about to enter college, planned to major in business. The M.B.A. (masters of business administration) degree was seen as the key to a successful career in corporate America. And the big corporations, which offered high starting salaries to new M.B.A.s, were where young people wanted to work.

Young Americans building careers in business or in professions such as medicine or law became known as young urban professionals, or "yuppies." The yuppie lifestyle involved total dedication to career and a willingness to work many hard hours in order to get ahead. The yuppie's goal was to have a successful career and the high standard of living made possible by that career. So many people were drawn to the yuppie lifestyle and yuppie values that *Newsweek* magazine decided to call 1984 the "Year of the Yuppie."

As more women entered the workplace, two-career families became common. Unlike during previous decades, many young married couples postponed having children until they had achieved financial security. The goal of making money replaced the ideals of social justice that had driven young people in the 1960s and 1970s. In 1985, Madonna released a song called "Material Girl." It seemed to represent the desire of many Americans to acquire more and more things. The lyrics went, "We are living in a material world, and I am a material girl."

Through the 1980s, women were fast becoming a vital part of the business world. Madonna was among the most successful female singers and businesspeople of her time. Her image affected not only styles of music, but fashion and lifestyle as well.

Dressing for Success

The conservative, ambitious mood in the United States during the 1980s was reflected in styles of dress that were similar to those of the conservative 1950s. Yuppies wore dark-colored business suits to work, which came to be called "power suits." A typical outfit for a professional working man of the 1980s consisted of a white dress shirt, silk tie, tailored jacket, and

Yuppies were characterized by their dark-colored, conservative attire (opposite). Both men and women dressed in so-called "power suits," which were considered the uniform for serious business-people in the 1980s. Meanwhile, the clothing worn by young people was becoming more outrageous. Influenced by stars such as Madonna and Cyndi Lauper and films such as *Flashdance*, many young women could be seen wearing "big hair" (above) and sexy, athletic-looking outfits.

leather wing-tipped shoes. A woman would also wear a tailored jacket, along with a below-knee-length skirt and a white blouse. It was important to yuppies that others recognize their success at first glance. Therefore, they wore expensive and noticeable items such as Rolex watches. And they spent a lot of money so that they could carry their cellular phones, first available in 1983, in fancy leather briefcases.

The Preppy Style

The yuppies' leisure-time wardrobe also reflected 1950s styles, as well as a concern with status. Yuppies favored the "preppy" style—casual wear that gave the appearance of wealth. Items of clothing had visible labels on them so that it would be clear that they were expensive. Typical clothes included classically styled jeans, khakis, or long shorts; shirts with conservative plaid prints or narrow stripes; white V-neck tennis sweaters; cable-knit sweaters; cotton turtlenecks; leather moccasins or penny loafers; Ralph Lauren shirts; and Calvin Klein underwear.

The Fitness Craze

Americans were very interested in physical fitness (below) during the 1980s. In fact, the video for one hit song, "Physical" by Olivia Newton-John, showed people doing an aerobic routine.

Yuppies were great believers in physical fitness and were concerned about their appearance. So they signed up for aerobic exercise classes in health clubs to improve their bodies. Many believed that being physically fit would help them compete more effectively in the world of business. The fitness craze in the 1980s led to a new look in fashion. Various types of exercise gear began to be worn as everyday clothing. These new styles included one-piece bodysuits, stirrup pants, leggings, tights, tank tops, bicycle shorts, and jogging shorts. These items were often made of new, snug-fitting fabrics such as spandex.

Punks, Rappers, and the "Grunge" Look

While the yuppies were busy building their careers and trying to impress people with their clean-cut, affluent style of dress, other young Americans were heading in a different direction. Teen clothing styles during the 1980s reflected several different influences. The punk style, which had originated in England during the 1970s, featured black clothing, leather jackets, and ripped jeans. American punks, male and female, wore earrings, sometimes several in one ear.

They also pierced their noses and other body parts. They dyed their hair in bright colors. Some wore their hair in a style known as a Mohawk, in which most of the head was shaved, leaving only some hair down the middle of the scalp.

Another trend in teen fashion featured oversized clothes and clothes that looked old. Faded denim became popular, as did the practice of tearing shirts. This ragged, secondhand, low-cost look, known as grunge, was the opposite of the neat styles worn by yuppies. The grunge look first became popular in Seattle, and then spread to the rest of the country. Another influence on teen fashion came from African-American rap singers. In addition to oversized clothes, rappers wore brand-name sneakers without laces, baseball caps turned sideways or backward, and sweatsuits.

Many young people in the United States and around the world rebelled against the conservative, materialistic values and styles of the yuppies by sporting the punk look. In addition to wild clothes, multiple earrings, and colorful hair, some had their hair cut into outrageous styles such as the spiked Mohawk (above).

Erno Rubik introduced his cube (right) in 1980. Within months, people were trying frantically to solve the puzzle. For those who had trouble, many books and guides went on sale, offering tips on how to complete the Rubik's Cube. One book explained in detail how to take the cube apart carefully and put it back together with the colors correctly aligned.

Rubik's Cube

In every decade, certain fads quickly take the country by storm. Earlier decades saw such fads as the hula hoop and the pet rock. In 1980, Americans became obsessed with a puzzle known as the Rubik's Cube. Erno Rubik, a Hungarian professor of architecture, had invented his cube in 1974. He had first come up with the idea as a challenge for his students. Once a person tried to solve the puzzle, he or she often could not put it down. People became hooked on the cube, spending hours at a time trying to solve it. By the end of 1981, more than 10 million Rubik's Cubes had been sold throughout the world.

Rubik's Cube was a six-sided cube that consisted of twenty-six smaller cubes. The cubes could be rotated in any direction. The object was to end up with a different uniform color on each of the six sides of the Cube. There were more than 43 quintillion (43,000,000,000,000,000,000) different positions possible for the smaller cubes. Of course, some people figured out how to do it. But many people could not, and it drove them crazy. As frustration mounted, a Cube Smasher became available. Advertisements said the Cube Smasher could beat the Rubik's Cube into 43 quintillion pieces! More than 100,000 Cube Smashers were quickly sold.

Pac-Man

Another fad of the early 1980s was a video game called Pac-Man. Like Rubik's Cube, Pac-Man had been invented during the 1970s. Namco Limited, the Japanese company that developed the game, based its name on the Japanese word *paku*, which means "to eat." The more dots Pac-Man

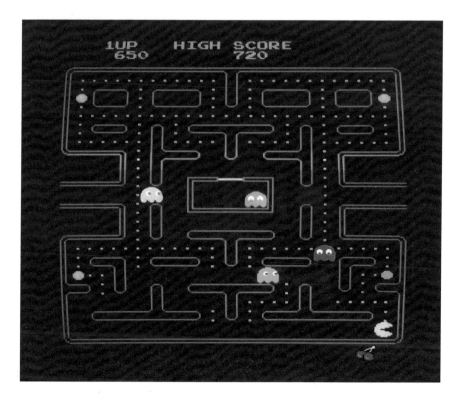

While people struggled to line up the colored cubes of the Rubik's Cube, many others lined up in video arcades to play Pac-Man (left). In addition to the original game, Pac-Man led to a series of spin-off games. Among these was Ms. Pac-Man, a character who looked just like the original, except for the bow in her "hair."

When Cabbage Patch Kids (right) were first introduced, they were often hard to find in stores. Parents could sometimes be seen running, grabbing, and even fighting to try to buy a Cabbage Patch Kid for their children.

Not only did each doll come with adoption papers that bore the company-given name of the Cabbage Patch Kid, but each would also receive a card on its first birthday from the company that made the dolls—that is, if the owner remembered to send in all the official paperwork.

devoured without being eaten by ghosts, the more points a player scored. Pac-Man appeared in video arcades in the United States in October 1980. Within eighteen months, Americans spent about $1 billion to rack up record scores. There were Pac-Man contests. Guidebooks such as *How to Win at Pac-Man* became best-sellers. Pac-Man soon became available in other formats such as a computer cartridge game, board game, card game, and puzzle. There was even a Pac-Man wristwatch version that could be played anywhere.

Cabbage Patch Kids

The most memorable toy of the 1980s was a doll with fat cheeks and a pinched nose known as the Cabbage Patch Kid. Xavier Roberts, a young Georgia sculptor, created the first Cabbage Patch Kid. He had come up with the idea after discovering soft sculptures at arts and crafts fairs in the South. Coleco Industries, a toy company, agreed to mass-produce Cabbage Patch Kids. Once these

dolls appeared in toy stores in 1983, children all around the country fell in love with them. At first, many people thought the dolls were ugly. Kids loved them, however, and many soon regarded the dolls as adorable. Each Cabbage Patch Kid was unique in some way—some had dimples, pacifiers, or different hairstyles. Each doll came with "official" adoption papers. Cabbage Patch Kids became must-have items. Millions of the dolls were sold, and Coleco had trouble keeping up with the demand.

New Age Music

In the 1980s, a new kind of music became popular, especially among yuppies. In general, this music, which came to be called New Age, tended to have a limited range of emotional expression. The music had a soothing effect on listeners, and was great for relaxation and meditation. For those who needed a temporary escape from stress, New Age music was just the thing. The pleasant-sounding music, whether acoustic or electronic, featured repetitive melodies that did not seem to go anywhere. Pianist George Winston and harpist Andreas Vollenweider were among the most popular New Age musicians. Critics compared it to elevator Muzak. Some said that New Age music put them to sleep.

Compact discs and players would eventually come to replace traditional vinyl records in most American households. Although they were more expensive to buy than vinyl, they often lasted much longer without scratching or warping. The CD also seemed to be better than the other alternative—audio tapes. With a CD, a listener could quickly choose any song on an album at the touch of a button, instead of waiting to fast forward or rewind.

Compact Discs

The compact disc, or CD, was first introduced in 1982. Suddenly, music fans were able to enjoy listening to their favorite music without hearing the scratches and other surface noises of vinyl records. The CD's crystal-clear sound quickly gained popularity. Some people insisted, however, that the CD sound was sterile. It lacked the warmth that they claimed they could detect on a vinyl LP. But most people preferred the CD. By the end of the 1980s, the LP was clearly on its way out. The CD was in.

Rock Around the Clock With MTV

Music Television (better known as MTV) began broadcasting in August 1981. For the first time, young people who had grown up with television and rock music could watch rock videos twenty-four hours a day. MTV was largely responsible for the growing popularity of music videos and new trends in music and dance. The 1980s saw the increasing popularity of break dancing, an acrobatic style of dance that involved spinning and touching parts of the body to the floor, and a tightly synchronized, almost robotic movement, featured in the music videos of artists such as Michael Jackson. The performers featured on MTV influenced the styles of music and dancing that were popular among young people. They also changed fashion, as teens copied the new trends seen in music videos.

Break Dancing and Rap

In the early 1980s, break dancing, along with rap music and graffiti, made up a cultural trend known as hip-hop. Break dancing had actually begun in the late 1970s, among Hispanic and African-American youths. It was a kind of competition to see who could come up with the most amazing moves. Skilled break dancers seemed to defy gravity as they spun around quickly on their back, shoulders, or head.

Rap music was a form of poetry set to rhythm. It gave young African Americans an artistic means of expressing their outrage at the many injustices experienced by ghetto youth. Rap music, which started in the late 1970s in the South Bronx, became popular with both white and black young

people in the 1980s. After years of resistance, MTV finally launched the daily program *Yo! MTV Raps* in the late 1980s, hosted by Fab Five Freddy. The show quickly became the most popular program on the network. Among the most famous rappers of the 80s were Afrika Bambaataa, Grandmaster Flash, Queen Latifah, Salt'n'Pepa, Tone-Loc, L. L. Cool J, and Ice T.

Graffiti Art

The various elements of hip-hop culture could all be seen as a form of protest. Graffiti art had begun appearing on the walls of buildings and on subway cars and buses in the 1970s, a time of upheaval caused by the unpopular Vietnam War and the Watergate scandal, among other problems. Young people from urban ghettos, who felt they had no chance to make it in the elite world of art galleries and museums, saw graffiti as a way to make society aware of their existence. Many people

Break dancing took great skill, balance, and coordination. Inspired by the wild moves of pop stars such as Michael Jackson, break dancers did robotic movements and spun themselves around with amazing precision.

considered graffiti art a form of vandalism that messed up public spaces. But by the 1980s, graffiti art was beginning to be recognized by some art critics as a serious form of artistic expression. Graffiti was even exhibited in art galleries. Among the most popular graffiti artists of the 1980s were Jean-Michel Basquiat, Keith Haring, and future MTV host, Fab Five Freddy.

Pop Music Superstars

In 1980, one question that had long been on the minds of music fans was settled for good. The Beatles—John, Paul, George, and Ringo—would never again make music together. That year, the life of one of the greatest stars in the history of rock—John Lennon—came to a tragic end. Lennon was shot and killed outside his apartment in Manhattan by Mark Chapman, a madman claiming to be a fan.

Many musical artists achieved fame and fortune in the 1980s. Some, such as Michael Jackson and Bruce Springsteen, had been performing and recording for a long time. But it was not until the 1980s that they became true superstars. In 1982, Michael Jackson released his album *Thriller*, which would eventually sell more than 40 million copies. In the next few years, a "Michaelmania" craze swept the world. Millions of fans rushed out to buy items associated with Jackson's image. They bought Michael Jackson posters, notebooks, key chains, caps, and T-shirts. Jackson earned eight Grammy Awards for *Thriller*.

Bruce Springsteen, known as the Boss, hit the jackpot in 1984 with the release of his album *Born in the U.S.A.* Jackson and Springsteen benefited from the broadcasting of their videos on MTV.

Many other artists, such as Madonna, also used videos to build a huge following. Madonna had a shrewd strategy for promoting herself. She changed her image a number of times throughout the 1980s to generate excitement about what she was doing. Her songs and videos were a mix of dance numbers and romantic ballads.

The artist known as Prince became a superstar in 1984 with his album and movie *Purple Rain*. Other big music stars of the decade included Cyndi Lauper, Whitney Houston, Billy Joel, Pat Benatar, Lionel Richie, George Michael, and Bon Jovi. Superstars of previous decades, such as David Bowie, Rod

Bruce Springsteen (below) had been playing his own kind of working-class rock for years before he became a major star in the 1980s. With his backup E Street Band, featuring saxophone player Clarence Clemens, Springsteen appealed to many Americans.

Stewart, Phil Collins, Steve Winwood, Tina Turner, and Aretha Franklin, achieved new success in the 1980s. Popular groups of earlier years, such as the Rolling Stones and the Grateful Dead, also continued to record and perform.

Music for a Good Cause

During the 1980s, many big names in the music business joined forces to raise funds for a variety of causes. In 1985, Michael Jackson and Lionel Richie wrote a song called "We Are the World." It was dedicated to raising money for famine relief in Ethiopia. In addition to an all-star chorus, the song featured solos by Jackson, Richie, Bruce Springsteen, Diana Ross, Bob Dylan, Ray Charles, Willie Nelson, Stevie Wonder, Paul Simon, Kenny Rogers, Tina Turner, Daryl Hall, Cyndi Lauper, and Huey

Lewis. The song raised more than $50 million in 1985. The money was given to relief organizations to be distributed in Africa.

On July 13 of that same year, a musical event called Live Aid raised $70 million for Africa. The fourteen-hour-long concert took place simultaneously at two locations— Wembley Stadium in London and JFK Stadium in Philadelphia. The concert was broadcast live to 150 countries. The audience was estimated at 1.5 billion people. The top acts included Elton John, Mick Jagger, Tina Turner, Bob Dylan, Keith Richards, Madonna, Hall and Oates, George Michael, and Elvis Costello.

Another 1985 benefit concert, called Farm Aid, took place on September 22 in Champaign, Illinois. The purpose of this event

The tragedy of widespread famine in Africa led to a positive development in the music world in the 1980s. Bob Geldoff (above) assembled artists from every category of music together to use their talents to raise money and awareness for the situation in Africa. In 1985, dozens of stars, including Phil Collins (far left, with Sting) of the pop group Genesis performed at the Live Aid concert that was held in Philadelphia.

was to make people aware of the problems faced not by people in Africa but by America's farmers. Organized by country singer Willie Nelson, it raised $8 million to $9 million for the nation's farmers. Performers included country stars Johnny Cash, Waylon Jennings, and Loretta Lynn, as well as rock artists such as Bob Dylan, Lou Reed, and Bon Jovi.

Movies of the 1980s: Spielberg and Lucas

Almost all the biggest movie hits of the 1980s featured spectacular state-of-the-art computerized special effects. At the top of the list was *E.T. The Extra-Terrestrial* (1982). Directed by Steven Spielberg, the film told the story of a lonely young suburban boy (played by Henry Thomas) who became friends

with an alien (E.T.) from another planet. The alien was a sweet, cuddly creature. Movie audiences, young and old, fell in love with him. *E.T.* eventually earned around $700 million at the box office worldwide.

Among the other top movies were other science-fiction fantasies such as George Lucas's *The Empire Strikes Back* (1980) and *Return of the Jedi* (1983), both sequels to his 1977 hit *Star Wars*. Lucas's Indiana Jones adventure films— *Raiders of the Lost Ark* (1981), *Indiana Jones and the Temple of Doom* (1984), and *Indiana Jones and the Last Crusade* (1989)—were all directed by Steven Spielberg.

Also high on the list of 1980s hit movies were *Ghostbusters* (1984), *Back to the Future* (1985), *Top Gun* (1986), *Rain Man* (1988), and *Batman* (1989). Almost all of them were big-budget, action-adventure or comedy films that appealed to Americans of the time, who were obsessed with better technology and flashy possessions.

Cable TV

A major change occurred in American television in the 1980s. Up until that decade, viewers could choose among three major networks—NBC, CBS, and ABC—and several local stations. Then, in the 1980s, cable television became available to a mass audience. Network broadcasting, which was supported by advertising dollars, was free to the viewer. But even though cable subscribers had to pay a monthly fee, cable television quickly grew in popularity. Suddenly, up to thirty channels were available. Americans appreciated the greater choice and variety in programming. Popular cable channels included MTV, VH-1, ESPN, HBO, Showtime, and TNT.

As cable television became more popular, the networks began to lose viewers. Because of competition from new cable channels, networks had to make changes in their traditional

Steven Spielberg's *E.T.* (opposite) won Americans' hearts with his glowing finger and his desire to "Phone Home." And Tom Cruise (above, with costar Kelly McGillis) sparked the interest of many young people in military flying with his role in *Top Gun*.

Don Johnson and Philip Michael Thomas, the stars of the action-packed cop series *Miami Vice*, encouraged men of all ages to copy their stylish clothing and slick hairstyles.

programming and scheduling. For example, in June 1980, Ted Turner began broadcasting news twenty four hours a day on his Cable News Network (CNN). In response, the networks had to devote more programming time each day to news shows. In 1989, CNN broadcast a live round-the-clock report of the events unfolding in Tiananmen Square in Beijing. Americans watched in horror as Chinese troops crushed the pro-democracy demonstration. And they admired one brave young man who stood up before an oncoming tank.

Popular Television Shows

One of the most popular television shows during the 1980s was *The Oprah Winfrey Show*. Oprah Winfrey's day-time talk show was a huge success because of the deeply personal nature of the interviews she conducted. She and her guests discussed controversial topics that touched the lives of many viewers. Other popular TV shows included the sitcoms *Cheers* and *The Cosby Show*, and dramas *L.A. Law* and *Dallas*.

Bill Cosby and the cast of *The Cosby Show* (left) broke television racial barriers. Often in the past, African Americans were seen on television only as struggling or unstable. The Huxtables—Cosby's television family—were affluent, well-adjusted, and happy, and viewers loved them.

What people watched on television affected all aspects of American culture. The rich wardrobes of the characters on *Dallas* and *Dynasty* influenced hairstyles, jewelry, and other fashions. The pastel T-shirts and sport jackets worn by the stars of the cop drama *Miami Vice* also popped up on ordinary people all over the United States, demonstrating the wide-ranging impact of television on everyday American life.

The baseball strike of 1981 would cause stadiums that had once been filled with enthusiastic fans to sit empty. Some fans, angered by the attitude of baseball players and team owners alike, would refuse for some time to watch or attend professional baseball games.

The Baseball Strike of 1981

The American love affair with baseball continued throughout the 1980s. But it was put to a severe test during the 1981 season. Major-league baseball players went on strike on June 12. The players and the team owners could not reach an agreement over salaries. The strike lasted until the end of July. The work stoppage caused the cancellation of 713 baseball games. Baseball players lost $30 million in wages, and team owners lost about $166 million in revenue.

The long strike not only led to bitter feelings between players and team owners but also made the fans angry. People who had always enjoyed either going to ball games or watching baseball on television became frustrated. Many wondered whether the fans would become so turned off that they might not return to watching baseball once the strike was settled. However, baseball survived. The fans did not desert their favorite teams. Indeed, by the end of the decade, 50 million fans were attending major-league games each year. And baseball revenues were more than $1 billion a year, including television deals.

The San Francisco earthquake of 1989 caused severe damage to buildings and roads in California (right) and even stopped a game in baseball's World Series.

Game Called on Account of Quake

Perhaps one of the most memorable baseball events was a game that had to be postponed. On October 17, 1989, the San Francisco Giants and the Oakland Athletics were getting ready to play game three of the World Series at Candlestick Park in San Francisco. At exactly 5:04 P.M., about half an hour before game time, the San Francisco Bay Area was struck by a severe earthquake, with a magnitude of 7.1 on the Richter scale. The entire stadium and the 68,000 fans in the stands were shaken by the rolling motion of the quake, which became known as the Loma Prieta earthquake.

Baseball fans all around the country were just sitting down to watch the game on television. They saw the ball players and their families rush out onto the field, where they would be safe. Fortunately, the fans were able to leave Candlestick Park safely, although there was some damage to the stadium. Other residents of the Bay Area were not so lucky. Buildings, freeways, and a section of the Oakland Bay Bridge collapsed. There were numerous fires. Sixty-three people were killed, and thousands were left homeless. Earthquake damage cost the area about $6 billion.

Sports and Politics

Many people feel that international sports competition should have nothing to do with politics. But unfortunately, during the 1980s, international politics often got in the way of sports.

In 1980, United States President Jimmy Carter declared that the United States would not participate in the twenty-second Summer Olympic Games in Moscow. This action was taken to protest the Soviet Union's invasion of Afghanistan. Many American athletes were very bitter. They had worked very hard, training for years to prepare themselves for the competition. Now some of them would never have the chance to compete in the Olympics.

Sixty-five other countries joined the United States in boycotting the Olympic Games in 1980. Four years later, the Soviet Union and its Communist allies retaliated by boycotting the twenty-third Summer Olympic Games, held in Los Angeles.

Because the Soviet Union had invaded Afghanistan, President Jimmy Carter withdrew United States athletes from the 1980 Olympics. Pictured below are the 1980 medal winners of women's gymnastics all-around: Nadia Comaneci of Romania, Maxi Gnauck of Grenada, and Yelena Daydova of the Soviet Union (left to right).

Ayatollah Khomeini (below, right) is greeted by a crowd of supporters upon his arrival at the airport in Tehran, Iran on February 1, 1979. Khomeini was the leader of the radical Iranian rebels who took a large group of Americans hostage in 1979. It would not be until the inauguration of President Ronald Reagan in 1981 that the hostages would be set free. The release of the hostages made many Americans hopeful about Reagan, a former movie actor (here, in a 1950s publicity photograph) who had become a successful politician.

The Movie Actor Who Became President

On November 4, 1980, Americans elected Ronald Reagan to be their next president. Reagan defeated President Jimmy Carter in a landslide vote to become the fortieth president of the United States. It was clear that people wanted a change. They associated Carter with the failure to free United States citizens who were being held hostage in Iran. They also blamed him for economic problems caused, in part, by higher energy costs. Meanwhile, Reagan emphasized patriotism and promised prosperity. Strangely enough, on January 20, 1981, the day of Reagan's presidential inauguration (and Carter's last day in office), Iran released the fifty-two remaining American hostages.

Some people thought it odd that an actor who had starred in many Hollywood B-movies and had hosted the television show *Death Valley Days*, had managed to become president of the United States. It was true that Reagan had gained political experience as governor of California. But after all, how could an actor know how to lead the most powerful nation on Earth? The fact is that acting skills can come in very handy for a politician. Reagan was popular with the voters because he was very effective in getting his message across. Known as the Great Communicator, Reagan was well liked, even by many who disagreed with his policies.

An Assassination Attempt

On March 30, 1981, shortly after giving a speech in Washington, D.C., President Reagan was shot in the chest by John W. Hinckley, Jr. Reagan's press secretary, James Brady, was also shot and seriously wounded. Reagan made an amazing recovery from his wound. And he became more popular than ever. Many Americans now saw him as a hero.

Reaganomics

Ronald Reagan served two terms in office, from 1981 to 1989. His economic policies tended to be conservative, favoring the interests of big business and the wealthy. President Reagan believed that, if taxes were lowered, people—especially the wealthy—would have more spare funds and would invest more money in corporations. If American businesses prospered as a result, they would, in turn, create more jobs and give pay raises to their employees. This was seen as a "trickle-down" effect that would help poor people. So in 1981 and again in 1986, Reagan reduced rates for corporate and personal income taxes. "Reaganomics," as this economic policy was called, was criticized by many as unfair to the poor. Many complained that the benefits never actually "trickled down" far enough to help lower-income people. However, Reaganomics was extremely popular among the yuppies and with businesspeople to whom it gave financial advantages.

The "Rainbow Coalition"

In 1984, the Reverend Jesse Jackson campaigned to be the Democratic candidate for the presidency of the United States. He was the first African American to wage a full-scale campaign to head a major-party ticket. Jackson appealed to Americans who had not benefited from Reaganomics— African Americans, American Indians, Hispanics, and other minorities, as well as small farmers and poor Americans who had been adversely affected by cutbacks in government support and services. Jackson referred to those groups supporting him as the "Rainbow Coalition." Jackson proposed a major public employment program, a renewal of federal spending on social services, expansion of civil rights, cutbacks in defense spending, and higher taxes for the rich.

For many years Jackson had fought long and hard for the expansion of civil rights for African Americans and other ethnic minorities. He became a well-known civil rights leader in the 1960s when he worked with Dr. Martin Luther King, Jr., and his Southern Christian Leadership Conference. He continued his civil rights activism throughout the 1970s,

forming Operation PUSH (People United to Save Humanity), an organization devoted to inspiring African-American high school students. In 1984, Walter Mondale won the Democratic candidacy for president but lost the election to Ronald Reagan. In 1988, Jackson waged another campaign in the Democratic primaries, finishing second to Michael Dukakis, who then lost the election to George H.W. Bush (the father of future President George W. Bush).

Street People: The Homeless Crisis

During the 1980s, the sight of people living on the streets of America's cities became more common. Many people wondered how this could be happening in the world's richest nation. But it really was not a mystery. Throughout the decade, the cost of housing continued to rise. Among the street people were those who had jobs but could no longer afford to pay their rent or mortgage. There were also many who were incapable of working. And many people had become dependent on government support that was no longer available. For these and other reasons, the number of homeless continued to rise. By the end of the decade, homelessness activists estimated that 2 million to 3 million Americans were living on the street, while the government's Department of Housing and Urban Development reported 250,000 to 300,000 homeless Americans. Whatever the exact figure, the numbers were growing.

The Stock Market Crash of 1987

President Reagan had promised to balance the budget. But his policies led to a dramatic growth in the federal deficit. In part, this was due to his huge increase in spending for defense programs. And it was partly due to lower tax revenues. Reagan's policies did lead to a lowering of the high inflation rates of the late 1970s and early 1980s. But by 1987, inflation was creeping up again, and interest rates were rising. During 1987, there was a wild burst of optimism in the financial

At the same time that upwardly mobile yuppies were watching their profits rise and fall in the risky 1980s stock market (below), hundreds of thousands of Americans were struggling just to live (opposite). These were the homeless, who could be seen on the streets of cities and even suburbs, carrying all of their belongings in bags or shopping baskets.

markets. The stock market surged to record highs. But the upward movement could not last. During the late summer, stock prices headed lower. And on October 19, which came to be called "Black Monday," the market fell 500 points, more than 20 percent. This was the biggest one-day drop since the stock market crash of 1929, which had set off the Great Depression. Luckily, the 1987 crash did not cause the same widespread panic and poverty as the Depression of the 1930s.

Star Wars

Ronald Reagan believed it was his patriotic duty to defeat communism. He referred to the Soviet Union as the "Evil Empire." Reagan poured hundreds of billions of dollars into a defense program known as the Strategic Defense Initiative (SDI). The purpose of this program, which became known as Star Wars, was to develop a space-based system of weapons that could shield the United States from an attack by Soviet nuclear missiles. Critics of SDI said the program would never work. Unfortunately, they were right. The technology was never successfully developed, despite all the money that had been spent.

The Tragedy of KAL007

Although the Cold War between the United States and the Soviet Union would wind down toward the end of the decade, the two superpower rivals still regarded each other with hostility and suspicion in 1983. The Soviets were particularly sensitive to any violation of their airspace, especially after an incident in 1978 in which a Korean airliner had flown hundreds of miles over Soviet territory before it was shot at and forced to land.

Soviet defense forces were authorized to stop any such intrusion by force. Unfortunately, on September 1, 1983, Korean Airlines flight 007 (KAL007) en route from the United States to Seoul, South Korea, strayed off course into Soviet airspace. After tracking the airliner, a Soviet fighter jet shot it down. All 269 passengers and crew members were killed. The incident seemed to validate President Ronald Reagan's characterization of the Soviet Union as an "Evil Empire," and Reagan referred to the tragedy as a "massacre."

The Iran-Contra Scandal

President Reagan's desire to defeat communism wherever it might arise eventually got him into trouble. In 1981, he had directed the Central Intelligence Agency (CIA) to help guerrilla forces in Nicaragua overthrow Daniel Ortega's leftist Sandinista government.

In the fall of 1986, Congress learned that an illegal, secret policy had been carried out by the Reagan administration to sell missiles to Iran in exchange for a release of United States hostages in the Middle East. The profits from the sale of arms were then used to fund operations of the guerrillas in Nicaragua, who were known as Contras. For a while, as Congress held hearings on the matter, it looked as if President Reagan might be impeached. However, others, including United States Marine Lieutenant Colonel Oliver North, were

The Iran-Contra scandal was a result of illegal actions in trying to remove the Communist government of Nicaragua. Several members of the Reagan administration were tried for their criminal actions, including Oliver North (below).

found to be responsible for the illegal activities. In 1989, North received a suspended three-year prison sentence and a $150,000 fine for his crimes.

The Cold War Ends

Ronald Reagan's massive military buildup probably played a key role in the eventual end of the Cold War between the United States and the Soviet Union. The Soviet Union could not afford the huge costs of building and deploying new weapons systems. Indeed, although the United States did not know it at the time, the Soviet Union was growing steadily weaker through the 1980s. Several decades of mismanagement and corruption had taken their toll on the Soviet economy. When Mikhail Gorbachev came to power in 1985, he called for *perestroika*, or restructuring, of the Soviet economy. His goal was to decentralize economic decision making. He also called for a policy of *glasnost*, or openness, in which Soviet citizens would be entitled to freedom of speech and assembly.

Gorbachev also wanted to improve relations between the United States and the Soviet Union—the two superpowers. Over the next few years, he and Reagan met several times. Their long talks often got bogged down in complicated details. But the two leaders were finally able to negotiate sweeping new arms treaties, which called for a major reduction in the numbers of nuclear missiles on both sides.

In December 1988, Mikhail Gorbachev announced that the Soviet Union was withdrawing many of its weapons from

Although he still hoped to preserve and renew the Communist form of government, Soviet leader Mikhail Gorbachev (above, at left) took great strides toward increasing the freedom of people living in the Soviet Union. His policies, however, would eventually help bring about the collapse of the Soviet Union and the Communist governments of the Eastern European nations that had been under its influence for decades.

The Berlin Wall, a symbol of the division between Communist and non-Communist countries in Europe, went up virtually overnight in August 1961. In 1989, the wall would be torn down by people from both sides—Communist and non-Communist—in a new symbolic gesture—the ending of the Cold War, which had lasted since the end of World War II.

Eastern Europe. Shortly after, the Communist governments of the Eastern European countries all fell. For years, Communist East Germany had kept people from leaving or entering the nation by force. The Berlin Wall was the most famous symbol of the closed Communist state. On November 9, 1989, East Germany opened its borders. The next day, East and West Germans together began tearing down the Berlin Wall, which had divided the city of Berlin since August 1961. Although many people around the world could hardly believe it, the Cold War finally seemed to be coming to an end.

Trouble in the Middle East

The 1980s turned out to be yet another decade of turmoil and war in the Middle East. In September 1978, there was good reason to be hopeful that there would finally be peace in the region. Egyptian President Anwar Sadat and Israeli Prime Minister Menachem Begin, with the help of United States President Jimmy Carter, had negotiated a peace agreement called the Camp David Accords. The agreement was signed in 1979. But in 1981, Sadat was assassinated by fanatics who considered him a traitor for holding peace talks with Israel. In the Middle East, trying to make peace proved to be a dangerous business.

In 1980, Iraq attacked its neighbor Iran in a border dispute. The resulting war lasted throughout most of the decade. Thousands of people lost their lives. Meanwhile, farther to the east in Afghanistan, the United States gave money and arms to guerrillas who were battling the Soviet Army. Finally, in 1989, the Soviets withdrew from Afghanistan.

The civil war that began to rage in Lebanon during the 1970s continued through most of the 1980s. Yassir Arafat's

Palestine Liberation Organization (PLO), which had been struggling for years to create a separate state for Palestinian people, attacked northern Israel from bases in Lebanon. In 1982, the Israeli Army invaded Lebanon in an attempt to destroy PLO bases. When the Israelis reached Beirut, the United States helped arrange a plan to allow the PLO to leave. United States Marines were sent to help evacuate PLO fighters. In April 1983, the United States Embassy in Beirut was blown up. Sixty-three people were killed. Then on October 23, 1983, 241 United States Marines were killed when the United States Marine headquarters in Lebanon was blown up. In 1984, United States forces were withdrawn from Lebanon.

The Ayatollah's Fury

In February 1989, the Ayatollah Ruholla Khomeini, the spiritual and political leader of Iran, issued a *fatwa*, or death sentence, for a writer by the name of Salman Rushdie. Rushdie had written *The Satanic Verses*, a novel in which he dared to make fun of the Islamic religion. Muslims around the world were outraged by the novel, and many supported the death sentence. Riots broke out in cities in India and Pakistan. Muslims in London, where Rushdie was living, threatened to

For decades, violence in the Middle East persisted mainly because of disagreements over ownership of the Holy Land. One of the leaders in the movement for peace was Egypt's President Anwar Sadat (above). In 1981, Sadat was assassinated.

kill him on sight. Rushdie was forced to go into hiding. He remained out of public sight for years until the *fatwa* was finally lifted in September 1998.

Women in Politics

British Prime Minister Margaret Thatcher (below) was one of a growing group of women winning major elective positions in the 1980s. Thatcher worked with American President Ronald Reagan to fight the spread of communism. Her efforts played a part in the downfall of the Soviet Union.

Margaret Thatcher, who had become the Conservative party's prime minister of Great Britain in 1979, led her country throughout the 1980s. Not only was she the first female British prime minister, but she became the first British prime minister to be elected three times. Known as the Iron Lady, she was a forceful leader who never hesitated to fight for what she believed in. When Argentina invaded the Falkland Islands in 1982, Thatcher sent naval forces to retake the British territory. After a three-week-long war, the Argentine forces surrendered.

In 1986, Corazon Aquino became president of the Philippines when she defeated President Ferdinand Marcos in an election. Her husband, Benigno Aquino, who was assassinated at Manila Airport in 1983, had been a political opponent of Marcos's. Marcos tried to steal the election from Corazon Aquino. But the people were outraged. Millions took to the streets to protest. Marcos and his wife, Imelda, were forced to flee the Philippines.

When Benazir Bhutto became prime minister of Pakistan in 1988, she also became the first female leader of a Muslim nation. Her father, Zulfikar Ali

Bhutto, a former prime minister of Pakistan, had been overthrown in 1977 by General Mohammad Zia ul-Haq, who sent Ali Bhutto to jail and later had him hanged. Benazir and her mother had to spend time in jail while Zia ruled the country. In 1988, Zia was killed in a plane crash. Benazir Bhutto then succeeded the same man who had ousted her father.

In the United States in 1981, President Ronald Reagan appointed Sandra Day O'Connor as an associate justice to the United States Supreme Court. She became the first female Supreme Court justice in United States history.

George Bush and the Invasion of Panama

In 1988, Americans elected George Herbert Walker Bush to be their next president after he had served for eight years as vice president in the Reagan administration. (His son, George W. Bush, would later serve as president for two terms between 2000 and 2008.) In December 1989, Bush ordered a United States invasion of Panama. Bush and his advisors had decided that it was necessary to remove General Manuel Noriega, Panama's leader, from power. Noriega had been indicted by the United States on drug trafficking charges. Although Noriega had been working for the United States Army and the CIA from 1955 to 1986, he had been caught selling United States secrets to Communist Cuba and the Soviet Union. During the 1989 invasion, Noriega was captured and brought to the United States. He would eventually be tried, convicted, and sent to prison.

The 1986 disaster at the Chernobyl nuclear power plant had devastating consequences for the Soviet Union, and caused fear in countries around the world that used nuclear power. These nations learned of the tragedy quickly, and did what they could to help the suffering Soviets (pictured).

Chernobyl: The World's Worst Nuclear Accident

On April 26, 1986, an explosion took place at a nuclear power station at Chernobyl, Ukraine (then part of the Soviet Union). The explosion ripped apart the nuclear reactor. Radioactive material scattered over an area of thirty-two thousand square miles. More than thirty people died in the explosion and fire. About one hundred thirty-three thousand people in the surrounding area had to be evacuated. Belarus, just north of Ukraine, received a heavy dose of radiation. Radioactive fallout from the explosion also affected many other parts of northern and western Europe. The final death toll from the disaster may reach as high as thirty thousand to forty thousand people in the coming years, as people develop cancer and other illnesses due to radiation exposure.

The Chernobyl disaster sent shock waves around the world. People wondered if the nuclear reactors in their own countries were safe. The antinuclear movement gathered steam. Although Americans had already experienced their own nuclear crisis with the Three Mile Island incident in 1979, more people in the U.S. and in other countries began to call for an end to construction of new nuclear plants after Chernobyl. They also pressed for those nuclear plants that had a history of problems and seemed to be particularly dangerous to be shut down.

As it happened, plans for building new nuclear power plants in the United States had already been put on hold—for a different reason. It was getting too expensive to build and maintain nuclear power plants. Other ways of generating electricity, such as burning fossil fuels like coal and oil, had become much cheaper.

Bhopal: The World's Worst Industrial Accident

The American-owned Union Carbide insecticide plant in Bhopal, India, was a disaster waiting to happen. And on December 3, 1984, it happened. There was a leak of toxic gas at the plant. As a result, an estimated thirty-five hundred to sixty-four hundred people died, and fifty thousand to three hundred thousand were seriously injured. Naturally, local residents were outraged.

The disaster pointed out the terrible mistake of building industrial plants in the midst of heavily populated residential areas. In 1989, Union Carbide agreed to pay the victims of the disaster and their families $470 million in damages.

A Sleeping Giant Awakens

One of the worst natural disasters of the 80s was the eruption of Mount St. Helens. The volcano in southwestern Washington, near the Oregon border, had been quiet for more than one hundred years. Then on May 18, 1980, at 8:32 A.M., it awakened with a mighty roar. Pressure had been building inside the volcano for almost two months, as indicated by the venting of smoke and ash. Then an earthquake caused a massive landslide of rock, ice, and snow on the mountain. The pressure in the volcano was released in a huge eruption as powerful as the explosion of five hundred Hiroshima-sized atomic bombs, according to one scientist. The eruption blasted away the top 1,313 feet of Mount St. Helens (about 8.8 billion cubic yards). The massive plume of ash from the eruption rose sixteen miles into the sky. The blast of heated gas flattened forests for up to fifteen miles. Rivers became raging torrents of mud, washing away bridges and homes. Some towns in eastern Washington were coated with up to seven inches of volcanic ash. Fifty-seven people died as a result of the eruption. By the evening of May 18, Mount St. Helens was a smoking crater. What had been a 9,677-foot-tall mountain was now only 8,364 feet high. The Mount St. Helens National Volcanic Monument was created in 1982 and has become a major tourist attraction.

On Sunday morning, May 18, 1980, a magnitude 5.1 earthquake shook Mount St. Helens (opposite). The massive volcanic eruption that followed would damage more than 250 square miles of land.

Exxon *Valdez*: America's Worst Oil Spill

On March 24, 1989, the oil tanker Exxon *Valdez* was sailing southward in Alaska's Prince William Sound. The huge ship was carrying a full load of oil when it ran aground on a reef. The result was one of the worst environmental disasters in

American history. About two hundred forty thousand barrels of crude oil (approximately 11 million gallons) spilled into the waters of the Sound.

The accident was a catastrophe for the environment of Prince William Sound. Untold numbers of fish, birds, and mammals died. The fishing industry of the local villages was wiped out. Beaches along hundreds of miles of seacoast were coated in oil.

The Exxon Valdez oil tanker spilled huge amounts of oil in the waters off the coast of Alaska. In addition to damage to beaches, thousands of helpless animals were killed or injured.

The Personal Computer: Machine of the Decade

Apple introduced an easy-to-use personal computer (PC) in the 1970s. During the 1980s, IBM and other companies jumped on the bandwagon and began selling PCs to American consumers. At first, people bought computers mainly to play games, such as Pac-Man. Eventually, with the development and availability of new software, word processing and spreadsheets became the most popular kinds of computer software. The computer age was beginning.

AIDS

While the 1980s saw the spread of AIDS, a horrible, incurable new disease, the decade also gave birth to amazing technologies such as MRI and the artificial heart. AIDS (acquired immunodeficiency syndrome) was first identified in 1981. The disease causes a breakdown in the body's immune system. The infected person is vulnerable to various other serious diseases, which eventually result in death. In 1984, researchers discovered that AIDS is caused by HIV (human immunodeficiency virus). By the end of the decade, hundreds of thousands of Americans were infected with AIDS.

The *Challenger* Tragedy

Americans were shocked and devastated by the untimely deaths of the *Challenger* crew (below, from left to right, top row: Ellison Onizuka, Christa McAuliffe, Gregory Jarvis, Judith Resnik; bottom row: Mike Smith, Dick Scobee, Ron McNair).

On January 28, 1986, millions of school children across America were watching a special television broadcast at their schools. Millions of other Americans were also watching. Christa McAuliffe, a high-school social studies teacher, was about to make history as the first ordinary citizen to travel into space. She was part of the crew of astronauts aboard the space shuttle *Challenger*. There was excitement in the air as the *Challenger* blasted off. But about seventy-four seconds later, excitement turned to shock and grief. The *Challenger* exploded, and everyone on board was killed. The tragedy served as a reminder that space travel is still extremely dangerous, and all who venture into space are true heroes.

MRI

Magnetic resonance imaging (MRI) and nuclear magnetic resonance (NMR) were new ways of viewing the inside of a person's body. The patient is placed in the field of an electro-magnet and then subjected to radio waves. The images produced give doctors much better information than X-rays. MRI and NMR are used in the diagnosis of brain tumors, spinal disorders, multiple sclerosis, and heart disease. Unfortunately, the new technology, when first introduced, was very expensive. Only large hospitals could afford it. By the 1990s, it would be cheaper and much more commonly used.

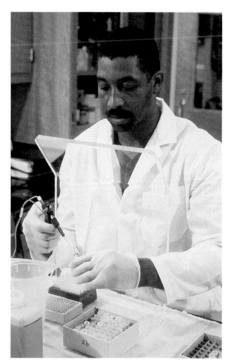

The Artificial Heart

In 1982, Dr. Barney Clark became the first person to receive an artificial heart to replace his own diseased heart permanently. Clark lived for 112 days after the device, known as the Jarvik-7, was implanted. William Schroeder, who also received a Jarvik-7, lived for 620 days. This was an amazing medical breakthrough, to be sure, but there were problems with it. The patient had to be hooked up to air compressors outside the body. And there was a constant danger of blood clots forming in the Jarvik-7. Eventually, doctors realized that the device could only be used as a temporary measure until a real heart was put in the patient. But there was hope that, one day, a self-contained artificial heart could be implanted that would allow the patient to live a normal life.

Acquired immunodeficiency syndrome (AIDS) was first identified in 1981. Within years, the terrible illness, which causes many mysterious complications, would claim thousands of lives. Throughout the 1980s, doctors and scientists raced to find better AIDS tests (above), a cure, or at least a plan for prevention.

The 1980s saw tremendous advances both culturally and technologically. The decade marked the dawn of the computer age, as home computer ownership began to soar. One of the most popular PC models at this time was the 64-kilobyte Commodore 64 (above). By the next decade, PCs would commonly possess hundreds of megabytes of virtual memory to go with gigabytes of hard drive memory.

An Amazing Decade

The 1980s were marked by remarkable discoveries and achievements in science and technology. It was also the decade that brought such tragedies as the *Challenger* disaster, the Exxon *Valdez* oil spill, Chernobyl, and AIDS to the attention of Americans and the whole world. Perhaps best remembered for unique music, fashions, and outrageous celebrity personalities, the 1980s were a time of triumph and tragedy—a time that is sure to continue to have an impact for many years to come.

Timeline

1980   **Ronald Reagan** is elected United States president; **Rubik's Cube** first hits the market; **Pac-Man** is first introduced; **John Lennon** is murdered by Mark Chapman; **CNN** begins broadcasting; United States boycotts the Summer Olympic Games to protest the Soviet Union's invasion of Afghanistan; War begins between Iran and Iraq.

1981   **MTV** premieres; Hostages held in Iran are freed; **Ronald Reagan** is shot in an assassination attempt; Major-league baseball players go on strike; Reagan appoints **Sandra Day O'Connor** as the first female United States Supreme Court justice; **AIDS** is first identified; Reagan orders the CIA to overthrow **Daniel Ortega**'s government in Nicaragua; Egyptian **President Anwar Sadat** is assassinated.

1982   Compact discs (**CDs**) are introduced; *E.T. The Extra-Terrestrial* premieres in theaters; **Barney Clark** receives the first permanent artificial heart; **Michael Jackson** releases his *Thriller* album.

1983   **Cellular phones** become available; **Cabbage Patch Kids** appear in toy stores, causing a frenzy among children and parents; **United States Embassy** in Beirut is blown up.

1984   *Newsweek* announces the "Year of the Yuppie;" **Bruce Springsteen** releases his *Born in the U.S.A.* album; **Prince** releases *Purple Rain*; The Soviet Union and other Communist countries boycott the Summer Olympics; United States forces leave Lebanon; **Indira Gandhi** is assassinated in India; Toxic leak occurs at Union Carbide plant in Bhopal, India; **HIV** (human immunodeficiency virus) is discovered to be the cause of AIDS.

1985   Madonna releases "Material Girl," echoing the materialistic sentiments of Americans; "We Are the World" debuts to raise money to end famine in Africa; **Live Aid** concerts are held to help African famine victims; **Farm Aid** concert is held to benefit American farmers; **Mikhail Gorbachev** comes to power in the Soviet Union and institutes reforms.

1986   Space shuttle *Challenger* explodes on January 28; Congress learns of the Iran-Contra scandal; **Corazon Aquino** is elected president of the Philippines; Nuclear power station at **Chernobyl** in the Soviet Union has a serious explosion.

1987   Stock market crashes on October 19.

1988   The Soviet Union announces the withdrawal of weapons from Eastern Europe; **Benazir Bhutto** becomes prime minister of Pakistan; **George Herbert Walker Bush** is elected United States president.

1989   **Tiananmen Square** uprising takes place in Beijing, China; **San Francisco** earthquake devastates parts of California; **Oliver North** receives a three-year suspended sentence for his role in the Iran-Contra scandal; **The Berlin Wall** is torn down in November, symbolizing the end of the Cold War; **Ayatollah Khomeini** issues a death sentence against **Salman Rushdie**, author of *The Satanic Verses*; **President Bush** orders the invasion of Panama to remove **Manuel Noriega** from power; **The Exxon *Valdez*** oil spill devastates Alaska's Prince William Sound.

Further Reading

Books

Jennings, Peter, and Todd Brewster. *The Century*. New York: Doubleday, 1998.

Judson, Karen. *Ronald Reagan*. Springfield, N.J.: Enslow Publishers, Inc., 1997.

Kallen, Stuart A. *The 1980s*. San Diego, Calif.: Lucent Books, 1998.

National Geographic Staff. *Eyewitness to the 20th Century*. Washington, D.C.: National Geographic Society, 1998.

Pick, Christopher, ed. *What's What in the 1980s: A Dictionary of Contemporary History, Literature, Arts, Technology, Medicine, Cinema, Theatre, Controversies, Fads, Movements & Events*. Detroit: Gale Research, Inc., 1982.

Sherrow, Victoria. *The Exxon Valdez: Tragic Oil Spill*. Springfield, N.J.: Enslow Publishers, Inc., 1998.

Twist, Clint. *1980s*. Orlando, Fla.: Raintree Steck-Vaughn Publishers, 1993.

Internet Addresses

In the 80s
http://www.inthe80s.com/index.shtml

The '80s Server
http://www.80s.com/default.html

White House Historical Association.
Ronald Reagan: Fortieth President, 1981–1989
http://www.whitehouse.gov/history/presidents/rr40.html

Index